Diving into Poetry Forms

Pamela Bergmann
Ruth Carter
Jeff Lucas
Carol Renfro
Constance Taylor
Nancy Verlinde

ISBN 978-1954896130 Paperback

Library of Congress Control Number: 2025917466

Design: Susan Cohen, wordsatwork.net

Susan Cohen is originally from Boston and now makes her home in Sweden. Sue specializes in freelance editing, translating, graphic design and poetry making. She is delighted to have shared in creating this book.

Cover Images:

Abstract Water Wave by elaelo, ID 336632364, DepositPhotos.com

Unreadable Hand-written Poems by Barsova, ID 423718822, DepositPhotos.com

Woman Continuous Line Drawing by SimpleLine, ID 427173236, DepositPhotos.com

fathompublishing.com
Fathom Publishing Company
Anchorage, Alaska
Printed in the United States of America

A Perfect Day to Read

Heavy clouds give way.
Rain, rain, rain.
Today's hike postponed.

Lune Poem by Pamela Bergmann

Image Credits in Order of Appearance

Interior with poppies and reading woman by Lizzy Hohlenberg, commons.wikimedia.org/wiki/File:Interior_with_poppies_and_reading_woman_(Lizzy_Hohlenberg)_905.jpeg

Wooden press box by RobC87, ID 755439448, DepositPhotos.com

Calligraphy, Quills, Ink Pens by Magnilion, ID 2205266425, istockphoto.com

Human Brain by microstockmilan, ID 54175005, Depositphotos.com

Opened door to dreams world by bestmanua_K, ID 5316259, Depositphotos.com

Greetings from a Great Country, Boston Public Library, commons.wikimedia.org/wiki/File:Greetings_from_a_great_country.jpg

Arctic Valley Fog by Constance Taylor

Chester Creek Trail by Constance Taylor

Overcast view by AntonMatyukha, ID 270359652 DepositPhotos.com

Swans at Potter Marsh by Constance Taylor

Gateway to all Nations by RobNow, ID 728083170, Depositphotos.com

Bald Eagle by Constance Taylor

Two Bald Eagles © Ephraim Ezekiel

Noatak River by Pamela Bergmann

Red Robin by Constance Taylor

Waxwing and Clouds by Constance Taylor

Salami Pizza Slice by memoangeles, ID 56862433 Depositphotos.com

Black Bear by Constance Taylor

Wine Bottles by Boarding2Now, 212283160, Depositphotos.com

White Sardines by Anthonycz, ID 58979129 Depositphotos.com

Alaska Salmon Caneries, commons.wikimedia.org/wiki/Category:Alaska_in_art#/media/File:Alaskan_Salmon_Canneries,_Title_Page_-_Alaska_Salmon_Cannery,_Kake,_Wrangell-Petersburg_Census_Area,_AK_HAER_AK,22-KAKE,1-_(sheet_1_of_2).tif

Spawning Fish, © Valeko, ID 13742531, Dreamstime.com

Steam by lineartestpilot, ID 20947787, DepositPhotos.com

Old Brass Pot by amnarj20066, ID 738401040, DepositPhotos.com

Little Boy with Chocolate by yupiramos, ID 259280884, Depositphotos.com

Tlingit Basket with Orca Motif by Unidentified Tlingit, commons.wikimedia.org/wiki/File:Tlingit_basket_with_orca_motif_c._1900_02.jpg

Orca Whales by Nancy Verlinde

Mountain Gorillas by Pamela Bergmann

Sitka Deer by Pamela Bergmann

Taj Mahal by Pamela Bergmann

Denali by Pamela Bergmann

Sandhill Cranes by Pamela Bergmann

Running out of Time, mtkang, ID 8584899 Depositphotos.com

Bengal Tigers by Pamela Bergann

Green Island Waves by Pamela Bergmann

House by JayaGPX, ID 730444870 DepositPhotos.com

American Dollars Falling by Begin Again, ID 351659746, Depositphotos.com

Cute Funny Puppies by lisi-note@yandex.ru, ID 378516390 Depositphotos.com

Beige Dog by Iridi, ID 397568998, Depositphotos.com

Black Dogs by Ruth Carter

Prismatic Human Cooperation Heart, @GDJ openclipart.org/detail/253651/prismatic-human-cooperation-heart-3-no-background

Democracy or autocracy symbol, © Dzmitry Dzemidovich, ID 221975847, Dreamstime.com

Evening Landscape - Tiffany Studios, commons.wikimedia.org/wiki/File:Evening_Landscape_-_Tiffany_Studios,_c._1910.JPG

Red-brested Nuthatch by Constance Taylor

Peaceful Garden by Carol Renfro

Mexican Bamboo by Carol Renfro

Seine boat by Constance Taylor

Royal Black Cat by Kudryashka, ID 223735270, Depositphotos.com

Cat by Carol Renfro

Cute Sleeping Cat by Kudryashka, ID 192145436, Depositphotos.com

Cat by Carol Renfro

Route 70 Highway Sign by by RexWholster, ID 538853250, Depositphotos.com

Relaxation by little_prince, ID 309311898,Depositphotos.com

Old-fashioned four legged TV by tuulijumqala, ID 2832780 Depositphotos.com

Hugging Emoticons by yayayoyo, ID 3915202 Depositphotos.com

Alaska [Camps at Kennedys Road House on New Gov. Trail, Thomson Pass], www.loc.gov/pictures/item/2016821825

Muir Glacier, Alaska by Thomas Hill, commons.wikimedia.org/wiki/File:Thomas_Hill._Muir_Glacier,_Alaska._Oakland_Museum_of_California.jpg

Family Sketch by Kudryashka, ID 38723227, Depositphotos.com

Alaska Siberia Statue by Wendy Kenny

Sunset over March by Sydney Laurence, commons.wikimedia.org/wiki/File:Sunset_over_March,_oil_on_canvas_board_painting_by_Sydney_Laurence,_c._1900,_Anchorage_Museum.jpg

Orange Sunset by Constance Taylor

Young on the Party by nuraschka, ID 13762354, Depositphotos.com

Contents

Introduction

This anthology is a collection of poems created during an eight-week poetry class held in the spring of 2025. Each week, after the class was introduced to several styles of poetry, the participants wrote poems following those forms.

This book includes poems composed and shared during the class. It holds word treasures found when poets enthusiastically dive into poetry writing.

Constance Taylor
Summer 2025

New Passion

Into the brink I jumped.

Loving every minute
Out of the blue, words come tumbling
Varied thoughts and phrases
Each unique and heartfelt.

Poetry is my new passion
Opening my eyes to another world
Ever challenging, thought provoking
Meanings sometimes hidden
Satisfying for the moment, an impulse to write.

Acrostic Poem by Pamela Bergmann

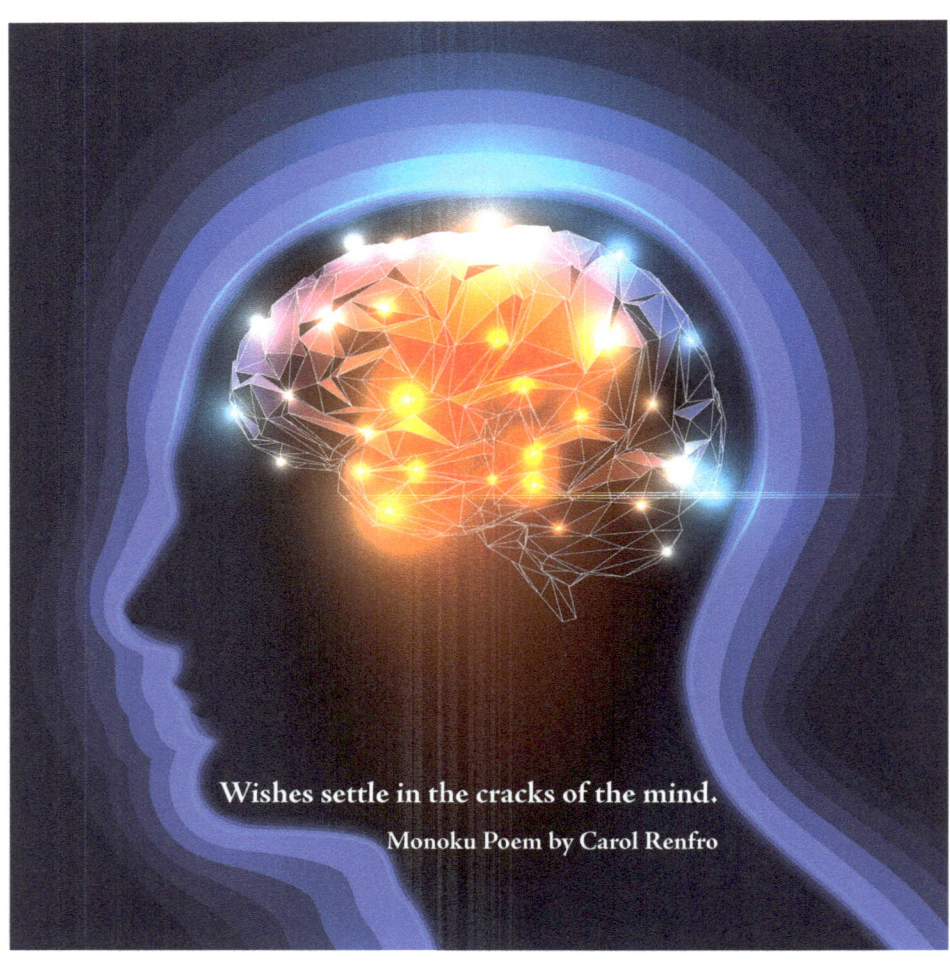

Wishes settle in the cracks of the mind.
Monoku Poem by Carol Renfro

Cleaning
Clutter
Dusty arrangements
Increasing daylight
Spring
Emptied boxes in piles
Memories

Elevenie Poem by Ruth Carter

I awake
Spring
Time to clean house
Dust
My senses heightened
In lengthening daylight
    I escape out the door

Pi Poem by Ruth Carter

3

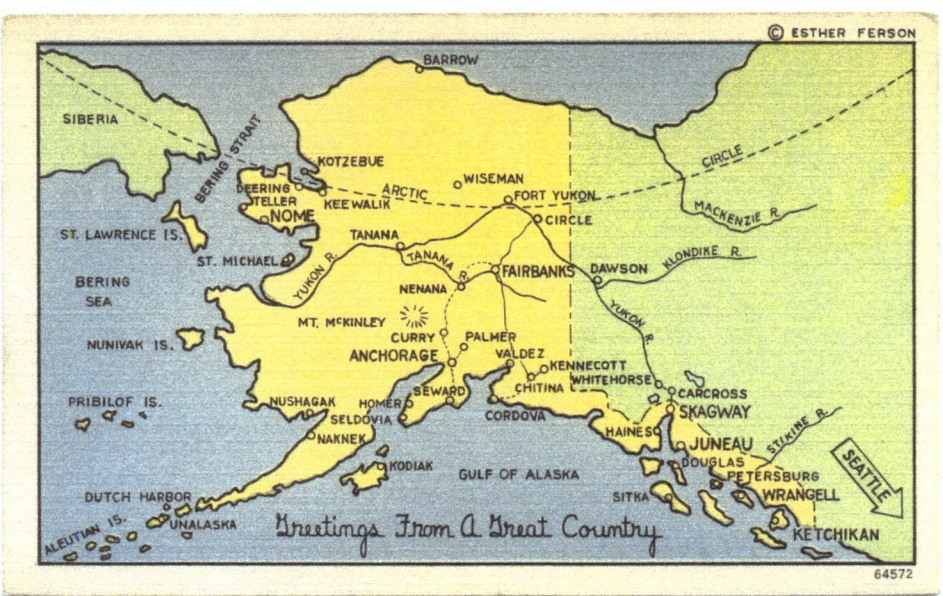

Alaska

Alaska a land of beauty and splendor
this is a place that stole my heart
consider no other state a contender
I'm here now and can never depart

This is a place that stole my heart
I hiked her hills and then her rivers
wandered mountains too mammoth to chart
her wonders always left me with shivers

Consider no other state a contender
California Washington no account
so I always will be a bitter-ender
Alaska's greatness is so paramount

I'm here now and can never depart
this is a place that stole my heart

Dave Poem by Constance Taylor

Hidden Trees

Golden trees, evergreen spruce

adorn the valley floor and hillside

beautiful in all their autumn splendor

yet even their brilliance fades beneath morning fog

as mist gently cloaks the landscape.

Free Verse by Nancy Verlinde

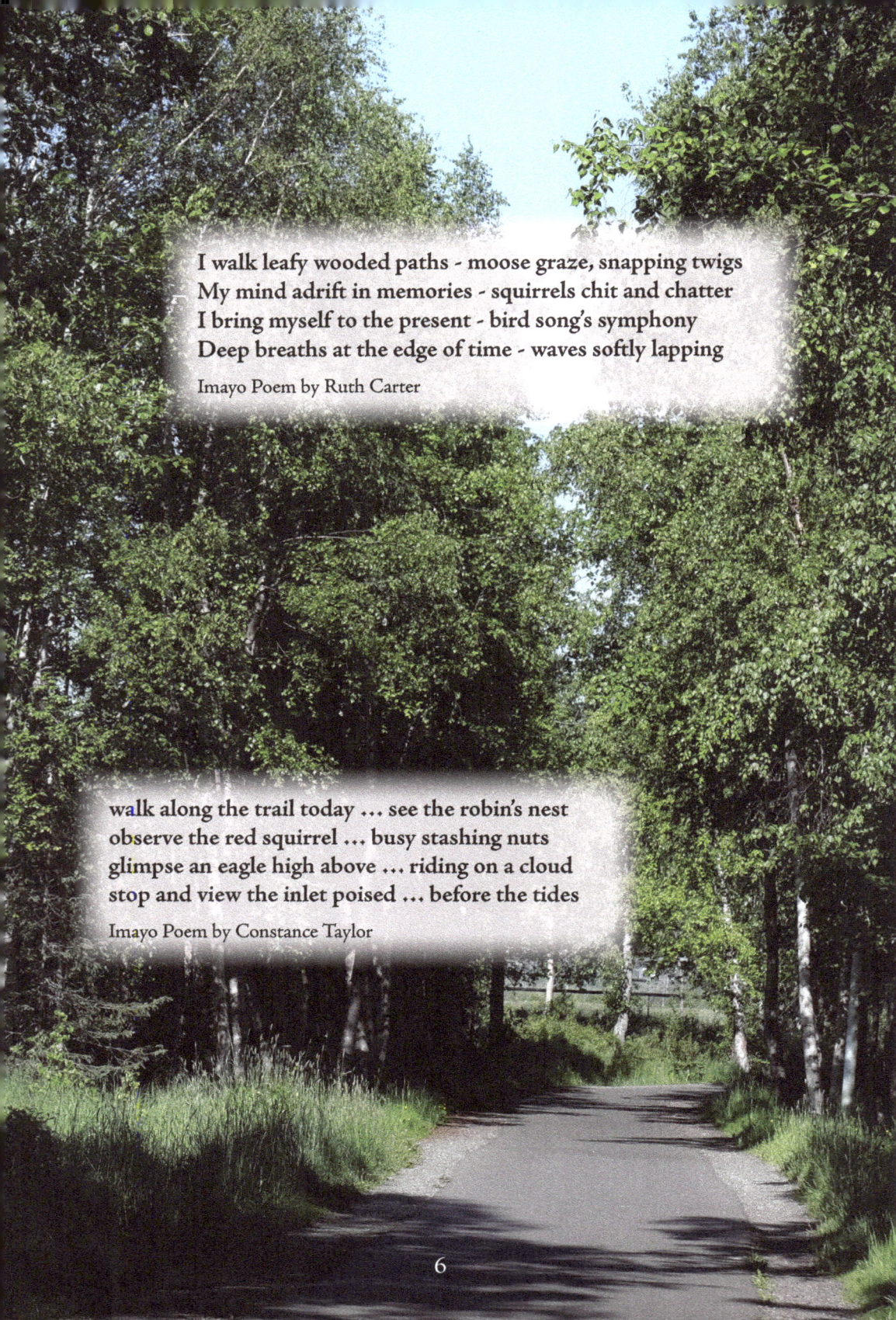

I walk leafy wooded paths - moose graze, snapping twigs
My mind adrift in memories - squirrels chit and chatter
I bring myself to the present - bird song's symphony
Deep breaths at the edge of time - waves softly lapping

Imayo Poem by Ruth Carter

walk along the trail today ... see the robin's nest
observe the red squirrel ... busy stashing nuts
glimpse an eagle high above ... riding on a cloud
stop and view the inlet poised ... before the tides

Imayo Poem by Constance Taylor

Marsh Visit

at the marsh today
for camera play
awesome
love the waterway
always want to stay
welcome
stroll down the walkway
watch ducks fly away
blithesome

Lia Poem by Constance Taylor

rain on marsh waters, trumpeter swans in a row.
A Monoku by Constance Taylor

The Eye of Xerxes

He never saw it coming
Flying beyond the heights of youthful dawn
Lifted upon kinetic points, resisting gravity
Javelin moving quickly
Zeroed on Xerxes eye

Pangram Poem by Jeff Lucas

Arctic Valley

Just north of Anchorage, Alaska,
the morning sun peeks over the mountains.
Bald eagles stand together on a tall tree
surveying the valley as they await
the sun's warmth on this winter day.
I hold the camera, capturing their serenity,
black bodies motionless,
only white heads move, twisting side to side,
watching the world come to life.

Location Poem by Constance Taylor

Fishing for Lunch

The eagle soars over river
    quiver.
Watching the floundering fish
    swish.
Swooping, soaring, zooming in
    on fin.
In the talon to take to his nest
    and rest.
Dinner is served
    well deserved.

Echo Poem by Nancy Verlinde

Daily Decision

Each
day we wake to
see
how rough the sea will
be. Should we kayak, or should we wait
until
the seas are calm again?

Pi Poem by Pamela Bergmann

Paddling the Noatak

Silty water.
Strong winds.
Sloughing banks.
Powerful current.
Endless meanders.
Whose idea was this?

List Poem by Pamela Bergmann

Alaska Birdfeeder

Starlings in their group
      always visit in a troupe.
Steller jays take whole nuts
      bury them in garden ruts.
Sparrows all varieties
      keep to their own societies.
Woodpeckers stop by the suet branch
      pounding at the greasy mass.
Nuthatches visit upside down
      perky in their breast of golden brown.
Magpies showoffs all
      amaze me with their gall.
Chickadees visit here for peanuts
      while I much prefer donuts.
House mouse underneath
      gathers all the birds bequeath.

List Poem by Constance Taylor

red robin in the grass
earth worms beware.

Monoku Poem by Constance Taylor

Waxwing

I sit on the patio
enjoying a quiet lunch
serenaded by birdsong
when along came a waxwing
hovering above me
keeping my attention
before stealing my pizza.

Pangram Poem by Pamela Bergmann

black
bear
fearful
fishing fiend
on nearby stream's bank
scans the waters so eagerly
he surely must be hungry seeking supper now
do not let him spot me or I must run
bear dinner does not sound like lots of fun

Fibonacci Poem by Constance Taylor

Company's Coming

Write a list,
check it twice.
Potato or rice
H'ors d'oeuvre
Special foods
Gluten free
Vegetarian
Steaks or fish
or chicken, a wish?
Oh dear, I'm stressed.
Which dessert is best?
Red or white? (wine that is).
Pop the cork.
Worry later.

List Poem by Nancy Verlinde

Bucket made of tin—

Fish with shiny fin—

Supper!

Very Short Poem
by Carol Renfro

14

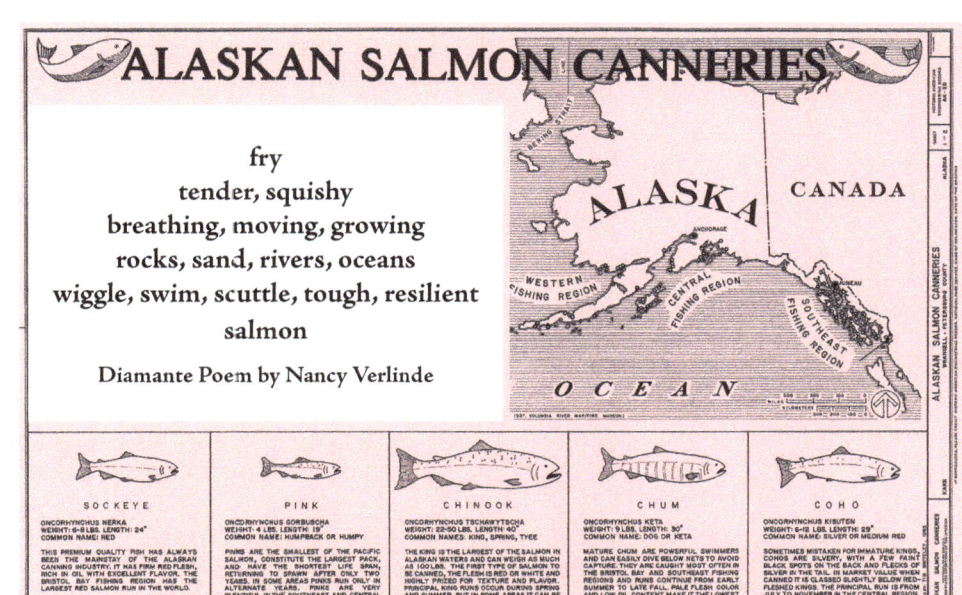

ALASKAN SALMON CANNERIES

fry
tender, squishy
breathing, moving, growing
rocks, sand, rivers, oceans
wiggle, swim, scuttle, tough, resilient
salmon

Diamante Poem by Nancy Verlinde

ALASKA   CANADA

OCEAN

WESTERN FISHING REGION
CENTRAL FISHING REGION
SOUTHEAST FISHING REGION

SOCKEYE
ONCORHYNCHUS NERKA
WEIGHT: 6-8 LBS. LENGTH: 24"
COMMON NAME: RED

THIS PREMIUM QUALITY FISH HAS ALWAYS BEEN THE MAINSTAY OF THE ALASKAN CANNING INDUSTRY. IT HAS FIRM RED FLESH, RICH IN OIL WITH EXCELLENT FLAVOR. THE BRISTOL BAY FISHING REGION HAS THE LARGEST RED SALMON RUN IN THE WORLD.

PINK
ONCORHYNCHUS GORBUSCHA
WEIGHT: 4 LBS. LENGTH: 19"
COMMON NAME: HUMPBACK OR HUMPY

PINKS ARE THE SMALLEST OF THE PACIFIC SALMON, CONSTITUTE THE LARGEST PACK, AND HAVE THE SHORTEST LIFE SPAN, RETURNING TO SPAWN AFTER ONLY TWO YEARS. IN SOME AREAS PINKS RUN ONLY IN ALTERNATE YEARS. PINKS ARE VERY PLENTIFUL IN THE SOUTHEAST AND CENTRAL ALASKAN FISHING REGIONS.

CHINOOK
ONCORHYNCHUS TSCHAWYTSCHA
WEIGHT: 22-50 LBS. LENGTH: 40"
COMMON NAMES: KING, SPRING, TYEE

THE KING IS THE LARGEST OF THE SALMON IN ALASKAN WATERS AND CAN WEIGH AS MUCH AS 100 LBS. THE FIRST TYPE OF SALMON TO BE CANNED, THE FLESH IS RED OR WHITE AND HIGHLY PRIZED FOR TEXTURE AND FLAVOR. PRINCIPAL KING RUNS OCCUR DURING SPRING AND SUMMER, BUT IN SOME AREAS IT CAN BE CAUGHT YEAR-ROUND.

CHUM
ONCORHYNCHUS KETA
WEIGHT: 9 LBS. LENGTH: 30"
COMMON NAME: DOG OR KETA

MATURE CHUM ARE POWERFUL SWIMMERS AND CAN EASILY DIVE BELOW NETS TO AVOID CAPTURE. THEY ARE CAUGHT MOST OFTEN IN THE BRISTOL BAY AND SOUTHEAST FISHING REGIONS AND RUNS CONTINUE FROM EARLY SUMMER TO LATE FALL. PALE FLESH COLOR AND LOW OIL CONTENT MAKE IT THE LOWEST PRICED OF ALL VARIETIES OF CANNED SALMON.

COHO
ONCORHYNCHUS KISUTCH
WEIGHT: 6-12 LBS. LENGTH: 29"
COMMON NAMES: SILVER OR MEDIUM RED

SOMETIMES MISTAKEN FOR IMMATURE KINGS, COHOS ARE SILVERY, WITH A FEW FAINT BLACK SPOTS ON THE BACK AND FLECKS OF SILVER IN THE TAIL. IN MARKET VALUE WHEN CANNED IT IS CLASSED SLIGHTLY BELOW RED-FLESHED KINGS. THE PRINCIPAL RUN IS FROM JULY TO NOVEMBER IN THE CENTRAL REGION.

shimmering
silver salmon
swim swiftly
sensing special
spawning sites

Tautogram Poem by Pamela Bergmann

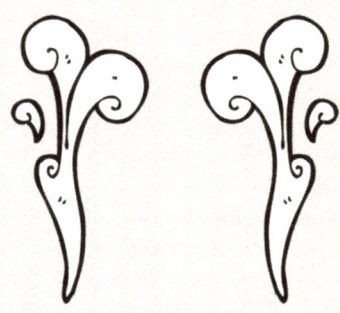

Saucepan made of brass--
Pork and taters hash--
Breakfast!

Very Short Poem by Carol Renfro

The candy box
Truffles!
Arranged in neat tiny rows
Sweet!
In a fine foiled box
Small coco flavored packets of heaven
All Mine!

Pi Poem by Jeff Lucas

Graced by a Visit

We look for deer.
Not to hunt, simply to see.
Green Island is home.

Camouflaged in forests.
Skittish by nature.
Open meadows avoided.

Late night visits.
Gone by morning.
Hoof prints on beaches.

One afternoon.
Through the cabin window.
Our wish, granted.

Narrative Poem by Pamela Bergmann

Ode to the Taj Mahal

Rising above the Yamuna River
your silhouette makes me quiver.
Taj Mahal, you take my breath away.
I must return another day.

Rising above the Yamuna River
your silhouette makes me quiver.
A tribute to everlasting love,
a deathbed promise from above.

Rising above the Yamuna River
your silhouette makes me quiver.
Pure white marble, precious stones,
dutifully holding your beloved's bones.

Rising above the Yamuna River
your silhouette makes me quiver.
Your stately beauty unsurpassed,
designed for eternity from the past.

Chant Poem by Pamela Bergmann

Longing for Mountains

I'm tired from cities.

The mountain's new-dropped summer snow is clear.

This is Mother Earth with all her glory.

The guide, the guardian of my heart, and soul.

Cento Poem by Pamela Bergmann

These lines are taken from Manvi Rawat, D.H. Lawrence,
Sumaiya Tapadar, and William Wordsworth.

Sandhill
cranes
fall
from
the
sky
like
rain.

Very Short Poem
by Pamela Bergmann

23

On Safari in India

Wake at 4:45 am.
Splash water on face.
Gulp coffee.
Grab daypack.
Meet driver.
Climb into jeep.
Drive to national park.
Pick up park guide.
Enter park.
Drive multiple miles.
Eat breakfast inside enclosure.
Stop for tigers.
Take photos.
Depart park at 11 am.
Return to lodge.
Gobble lunch.
Meet driver at 2:30 pm.
Return to park.
Pick up guide.
Drive multiple miles.
Stop for tigers.
Take photos.
Leave park at 6 pm.
Return to lodge.
Eat dinner.
Download photos
Charge batteries.
Write journal.
Collapse into bed.
Repeat the next day.

List by Poem Pamela Bergmann

The Tiger

We first see the tiger in the grass,
then silently moving into view.
The size and sleekness of its body
draws our attention to its power.

Then silently moving into view,
energy rippling through its body
draws our attention to its power
as it lies down to drink water.

Energy rippling through its body,
unconcerned with our company
as it lies down to drink water.
We first see the tiger in the grass.

Pantoum Poem by Pamela Bergmann

Since You've Been Gone

> Each day I'm faced
> with decisions to make
And still I dither.
> I'm challenged to choose
> one over another
And still I dither.
> It causes me angst,
> deciding right and wrong
And still I dither.
> But decide I must,
> for life goes on
And still I dither.

Chant Poem by Ruth Carter

Love. Laughter. Longing
Your life was too short. Come back!
And haunt this old house.

Haiku by Ruth Carter

Undecided

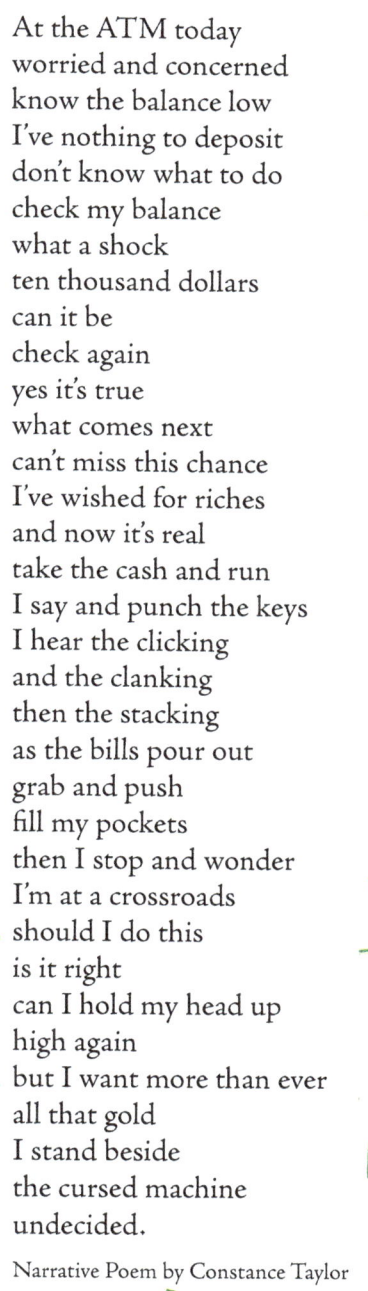

At the ATM today
worried and concerned
know the balance low
I've nothing to deposit
don't know what to do
check my balance
what a shock
ten thousand dollars
can it be
check again
yes it's true
what comes next
can't miss this chance
I've wished for riches
and now it's real
take the cash and run
I say and punch the keys
I hear the clicking
and the clanking
then the stacking
as the bills pour out
grab and push
fill my pockets
then I stop and wonder
I'm at a crossroads
should I do this
is it right
can I hold my head up
high again
but I want more than ever
all that gold
I stand beside
the cursed machine
undecided.

Narrative Poem by Constance Taylor

Puppies, puppies everywhere
Tails wagging in the air
Noses following the ground
With attention spans a minute long

Some are here and some are there
Sometime they seem everywhere
Licking, whining, growling too
Sometimes stepping in their poo!

They are active and move a lot.
Then suddenly they are NOT
Puppies puppies everywhere
snoozing still and on the floor

Nasher Poem by Jeff Lucas

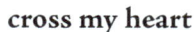

cross my heart

if i had opposable thumbs
i would open the fridge
and dine on rich foods

if i had opposable thumbs
i would open the pantry
that holds treats galore

if i had opposable thumbs
i would get into closets and drawers
where riches and treasures are stored

if i had opposable thumbs
i would still be a very good dog
really and truly i would

Chant Poem by Ruth Carter

Oscar

faithful, loyal, cheerful, friend
companion of my younger years
loved boat rides, doggy treats, woodland walks
and never feared sea lions or black bears
loved to see mallard ducks and Sitka deer
lived his life in Prince William Sound
Labrador Retriever

Bio Poem by Constance Taylor

Squirrel!
Dog
Sleeps soundly
Tightly curled ball
Dreaming of new adventures
Woof!

Lune Poem by Ruth Carter

Lucky dog
Precious bone to gnaw
Found treasure

Narrative Poem by Ruth Carter

each chord a note
but only together a melody

Very Short Poem by Constance Taylor

Democracy…Autocracy

Democracy
equality, respect
uplifting, assisting, celebrating
constitution, laws. Dysfunction, crimes
purging, gaslighting, self-dealing
greedy, cruel
Autocracy

Diamante Poem by Pamela Bergmann

sunrise
youthful energetic
glowing growing enlightening
birdsong meditation coffee stretches
waning settling darkening
steady aged
sunset

Diamante Poem by Ruth Carter

The Garden

The squirrel looks down from his place on the tree
While the nuthatch on the trunk goes headfirst down
The breeze in the garden lifts the bee
And the wren on a limb makes her nest neat and round.

The nuthatch on the trunk goes headfirst down
While the cardinal in red lifts his proud head
And the wren lines her nest with soft down
And the blackbird flashes his shoulder flag of red.

The breeze in the garden lifts the bee
While the blossoms expand to the light of the sun
The hummingbird hovers near the leaves of the tree
And the anole expands his pink throat, watching the fun.

And the wren on a limb makes her nest neat and round
While the nuthatch on the trunk goes headfirst down.

Dave Poem by Carol Renfro

Tomato Plant

I won't give up, you know
You're in the best spot to grow
Give it your all, my little plant
To be a Roma, don't say you can't

Nashers Poem by Nancy Verlinde

Weeds

The garden was in a frenzy
The weeds were sprouting everywhere
Unaware that spring was weeks away
It was not their time to dazzle.

Young seedlings still in peat pots
justified their existence
From the green house to the fertile soil
Before the warmth of spring.

Verily, I ask can this be true
The weeds will make room
For the fruits of my tender care
Secretly, quietly, unfolding.

Narrative Poem by Nancy Verlinde

showers for flowers
downfalls for roots

Nasher Poem by Carol Renfro

gardening
weeds
coarse, ugly
pull, annihilate, obliterate
seeds, seedlings, leaflets, buds
grow, flourish, water
dainty, tender
flowers

Diamante Poem by Carol Renfro

lavender
purple blossom
begets gray seeds
gathered in velveteen sachet

Elevenie Poem by Constance Taylor

Maintaining
the Mexican Bamboo

Clean the plot.
Cut brown stem at the base.
Break and flatten.
Break and flatten.
Pick up hollow pieces.
Pick up more hollow pieces.
Rake all around.
Pull loaded tarp to the road.
Repeat.
Wait.
Wait some more.
There! A tiny knob!
A green shoot!
Many green shoots!
Hollow green stems.
Dainty red and white flowers!
More red and white flowers!
Summer.
Autumn.
Brown leaves.
Hollow brown stems.
Repeat!

List Poem by Carol Renfro

Salmon Fishing Day

5am alarm
Wake the crew
Check the engine oil and water
Fire up
Anchor pull
Underway
Get in line at the point
Now it's our turn
Set the net
Pull it back
Got a few humpbacks
Set the net again, again, again
And again as day grows late
Keep watching up the beach
The current turns
Here the jumpers come
Success at last
Where's the tender?
Get in line
Unload
Quick dinner
Where's my bunk?

List Poem by Constance Taylor

Princess in the Night

The cat brushes her tail with her tongue.
She lifts her head and listens to the night.
Cat princess, she walks beneath the moon,
Black and gray she slides through the light.

She lifts her head and listens to the night.
Her eyes gleam, her paws seek soft places.
Black and gray she slides through the light,
Bushes of gardenias disclose their white faces.

Her eyes gleam, her paws seek soft places,
Her ears twitch, hiding secret fun.
Bushes of gardenias disclose their white faces.
The cat brushes her tail with her tongue.

Pantoum Poem by Carol Renfro

Dear Spooks

You purr so nicely on my lap
curled round as a river on a topo map.
Your eyes are shut, your body still,
you know I'd never wish you ill.
I have work to do, poems to write
that must be finished before the night.
It's never right to interrupt a catnap,
still I must put on my thinking cap.
Your friend, Connie

Epistolary Poem by Constance Taylor

Just south of 70°
North of 60°
Lies a patch of time that I call home
The decade of my retirement
Casual hobbies
Grandchildren and puppies
Travel to places only dreamed of
And time spent with my mother
Gazing into my 70th decade

Location Poem by Jeff Lucas

Hair
Gray
It's okay.
The real me
Remembers thick brown tresses, flowing in the sunlight.
Memories of youth, vibrant and lovely, flashbacks of life.
Gray hair and all, it's still me in the flesh, smiling and living life
in gratitude and sweet bliss.

Fibonacci Poem by Nancy Verlinde

Friends

In soap opera
Friends
Live in flesh and blood
We share episodes of make believe
We laugh
Appreciating what's real

Pi Poem by Nancy Verlinde

To Lydia Missouri Althatine Elizabeth Ward Flowers

Dear Lydia,
I want to thank you for the time you spent
with your grandson.
The room that you provided for him in the loft.
A young boy who to you was lent
even though the sheets could not be soft.
You lived in the mountains when times were hard.
You had other souls to tend.
And families struggled and roads weren't tarred
and fields were pushed by the wind.
The boy grew up, strong and bold.
He fought for his country and built a fold
for a wife and children you never knew.
And sadly, they never knew you.
With love and regret,
Your great-granddaughter.

Epistolary Poem by Carol Renfro

42

To Daniel

Rugged gray and white mountains grab the
viewer's attention to this landscape painting.
Four people spend moments and hours together
each in his or her own way.
The man wields his fishing pole,
the woman her camera,
the girl reads a book sitting on the picnic table bench,
the little boy floats a plastic boat in the lake.
The grown boy paints the picture,
catching the memories of a little family
in a large land.

Ekphrastic Poem by Carol Renfro

Drifting Sounds

The voice of my mother–
The voice of my father–
My sister speaking into the ears of her horse
       (which was really a tire swing)–
My brother slapping cards as he played
       war with his friends–
Me and my gang with our bikes at the gully
       by the dogwood tree in the woods–
Are these really sounds or only memories?
Either way they are beautiful.

Free Verse on Sounds Poem by Carol Renfro

Family

He gazes at the portraits, his family dear.
He whispers every name, each precious name clear.
He thinks of each daughter, his sons claim his thoughts.
But the image of his wife lives deep in his heart.

Imayo Poem by Carol Renfro

The Man

Howard

Quintessential man, dreamer, explorer, pilot

Lover of soaring high above the clouds

Freedom escaping the bonds of earth, no ties or restraints

His fears were few, he was bold in the throes of adversity

He wanted to see the world and he did

He's watching from the great hangar out west

My Dad – Howard Hunt

Bio Poem by Nancy Verlinde

Winter Comes

Snow arrives after a long silence. (Nancy Willard)

The winter evening settles down. (T.S. Eliot)

I went out at night alone. (Sara Teasdale)

Alone I stare into the frost's white face. (Osip Mandelstam)

As cars pass, laboring through the slush,
   a rabbit has stopped on the gravel driveway. (Authur Sze)

As I in hoary winter's night stood shivering in the snow. (Robert Southwell SJ)

My fingers are bitten with frost. (Rick Noguchi)

I paused and said, 'I will turn back from here.' (Robert Frost)

At home, in my flannel gown, like a bear to its floe. (Randall Jarrell)

The space heater glowing orange
   as it warms the floor near my feet. (James Crews)

Cento Poem by Constance Taylor

The sun sets in relative time
Disappearing and blazing orange
In another place and time
She shines brightly and warms the mind

Disappearing and blazing orange
Sundogs glow around her form
She shines brightly and warms the mind
A promise certain and a path to find

Sun Dogs glow around her form!

Pantoum Poem by Jeff Lucas

Dance of Life

Dance to the beat of your own drum
Life's too short to sit on the side
Big smile, happy thoughts, no glum
Enjoy it all, it's a great ride

Life's too short to sit on the side
Full tilt boogie, live on the edge
You won't regret the fantastic ride
It's vastly better than sitting on a ledge

Big smile, happy thoughts, not glum
Mark my words, my friend, it's true
Let's drink some wine squeezed from plum
Let's take a chance and stick like glue

Enjoy it all, it's a great ride
Time zooms by at the speed of light
No regrets, choose not one side
Release your soul to take flight

Enjoy it all, it's a great ride
Life's too short to sit on the side

Expanded Dave Poem by Nancy Verlinde

48

Poetry Forms

Acrostic – First letter of each line creates a word, phrase, or sentence reading down with no restrictions on line lengths or syllables.

Bio – Concise biography of a specific person or individual creature.

Cento – Type of "found" poetry composed of verses or passages taken from one or more other authors, placed in a new form or order with the author identified at the end of each line or in a single line after the poem. Cento is also called a Patchwork poem.

Chant – Repetitive lines that form a chant.

Dave – Four stanzas comprised of three stanzas with four lines each and a final stanza being a two-line couplet. Uses an ABAB rhyme scheme where the second stanza starts with second line of the first stanza; the third stanza starts with the third line of the first stanza; the fourth stanza starts with fourth line of the first stanza; and the final couplet is the fourth line of the first stanza and first line of second stanza.

Diamante – Seven lines arranged in the shape of a diamond beginning with the subject at the top of the diamond and ending with a totally different, sometimes opposite, subject at the bottom. The following rules apply: first line is a noun or single word; second line is two adjectives; third line is three verbs; fourth line is four nouns; fifth line is three verbs; sixth line is three adjectives; and last line is a noun or single word.

Echo – Each line ends with a repeat of the final syllable(s).

Elevenie – Eleven words in five lines. First line is one word, a noun; second line is two words describing the noun; third line is three words explaining the where and how of the noun; fourth line is four words with further explanation; and fifth line is one word, the outcome or conclusion.

Ekphrastic – Visual art is explored and resulting poem can be in any form, rhymed or unrhymed.

Epistolary – Verse letter or letter poem written to a public or private person or sometimes an animal.

Fibonacci – Syllables in each line must equal the sum of the syllables in the two previous lines; e.g., 1, 1, 2, 3, 5, 8, 13, 21, and so on. Based on the Fibonacci sequence used in mathematics.

Free Verse – Open poetry that does not use a regular meter or rhyme, usually following the rhythm of natural or irregular speech.

Haiku – Japanese short, unrhymed poem traditionally consisting of three lines with a syllable pattern of 5-7-5.

Imayo – Four-line Japanese form with twelve syllables in each line. Each line is split with a pause indicated by punctuation between the first seven and the final five syllables.

Lia – Nine-line French medieval lyric poem, often about adventure or romance with an AABAABAAB rhyme scheme. Rhyming A lines are five syllables; rhyming B lines are two syllables.

List – List of items, events, people, words, or other inventories typically without transitional or connecting phrases. May be any length or rhyme scheme or without rhymes.

Location – First word is "Just" and the first line(s) describe a location with the rest of the poem describing an action occurring at that location. May be any style, length, or rhyme scheme.

Lune – Also known as American haiku with a syllable pattern of 5-3-5 with rhymes not required.

Monoku – Single horizontal line noted for brevity and clarity.

Narrative – Story that does not need to rhyme and may be short or long.

Nashers – Couplets of any length, featuring comical rhymes.

Pantoum – Four-line stanzas with the second and fourth lines of each stanza serving as the first and third lines of the next stanzas. The last line is often the same as the first.

Pangram – Sentence containing every letter of the English alphabet.

Pi – Number of syllables in each line matches the digits in the mathematical constant "pi," which is 3.1415926. For example, Pi poems with seven lines would have this pattern: three syllables in line one, one in line two, four in line three, one in line four, and so on.

Tautogram – Every word starts with the same letter.

Very Short Poem – Single phrase or sentence noted for brevity and clarity in a single horizontal line, multiple lines, or artistically formatted.

Poets

Pamela Bergmann grew up on a farm in Nebraska, but migrated north to Alaska over forty years ago, where she fell in love with the landscapes, wildlife, and people. An avid traveler and photographer, after retiring from public service, she began sharing photographs, stories, and poems via her website at pamelabergmann.net. Twice a Pushcart Prize nominee, her work has been published in *Alaska Women Speak, Poetry Breakfast, Cirque, Anchorage Daily News,* and UCSF MERI Center Poetic Medicine Anthology.

Ruth Carter moved to Anchorage, Alaska, from Denver, Colorado and never looked back. She is captivated and held captive by the beauty of Alaska.

Jeff Lucas is a retired insurance professional who lives in Alaska. He is a husband/grandfather trying to stay relevant to those he loves.

Carol Cole Renfro received a degree in English from Agnes Scott College (she thanks her wonderful parents!) and a master's in Library Science from Emory University, which led her to her occupation as a librarian. Love of family, especially her children, reading, music, piano, singing, sewing and other crafts, teaching children and directing choirs in church, flower gardening and drives through God's beautiful countryside with her husband and camera have colored the days of her life, many of them with sunshine. She is thankful.

Constance Taylor left California to become an Alaska commercial fisherman. She fished for twenty years in Prince William Sound before settling in Cordova to become a printer and art gallery owner. Later, she moved to Anchorage to work as a paralegal, auctioneer, and bookkeeping consultant. Now she's a photographer, author and publisher. Her poetry has been published in *The Stafford Challenge 2024-25 Anthology, Alaska Women Speak, Lombardi Voices,* and *Poems that Flow Through Us.*

Nancy Verlinde grew up on a homestead near Anchorage, Alaska. She graduated from East Anchorage High School and attended the University of Alaska in Fairbanks. She co-authored the memoir *Saga of An Aviation Survivor* and has had numerous stories and poems published in *Alaska Women Speak.*

www.ingramcontent.com/pod-product-compliance
Lightning Source LLC
Chambersburg PA
CBHW041630140626
46547CB00032B/2545